UNCOMMON LEADERSHIP

What the Church Needs Most

Written by: Walter Robertson, III

All scripture reference from King James Version Bible unless
otherwise stated.

ISBN NO. 978-1-943409-86-0

Printed in the United States of America

This book is dedicated to the leaders who were called radical simply for being

UNCOMMON.

Reviews

Pastor Jake Sanders, III

"In this book, Uncommon Leadership, Pastor Walter Robertson encourages his readers that it is possible to be uncommon and still be unique, it is possible to be uncommon and still be anointed, it is possible mu brothers and sisters to be uncommon and still be called for such a time as this. As a 25-year-old young man who is currently in my second year of pastoring this book has encouraged me to embrace my true and authentic self while going forth knowing that there is nothing wrong with being an uncommon leader. The various chapters outlined in this book will indeed push you forward as you become and live out your uncommon leadership abilities."

Min. Angie Taylor-Reames, Author

This book has blessed me tremendously. The amazing thing about the contents are the versatility of the delivery. What I mean by that is, this amazing book is able to be used in both the spiritual and secular leadership venues. Although, one may assume it is just for the church wall, it is designed for the church as a whole, because individually we make up the "church." There are so many amazing tips and leadership thoughts that I am able to apply to my life, as I am more than confident will assist me in being successful. Wonderful job, Pastor Walter Robertson, you have done it again. Your experience in leadership is already blessed my life and may your work continue to bless those that you connect with, mentor, and lead.

Table of Contents

Introduction

Looking at the horizon and seeing the church of today you quickly realize that this isn't your grandma's church. Something has changed. Pastors have relaxed and are now presenting themselves in a manner that humanizes them. They have put away the three-piece suits and have replaced them with casual attire or better yet with denim and tee shirts, and they are being embraced more than ever before.

Pastors like Steve Furtick, Samuel Rodriguez, Dr. Matthew Stevens, Dr. Jamaal Bryant and a plethora of others have proven that you can be "**Uncommon**" and still be anointed. For years the church has defined what a Pastor/Leader should look like, should dress like, or should sound like, but

God has risen up a generation of uncommon leaders who have broken the traditional church mold of leaders. This new generation of uncommon leaders is taking the world by storm for the Kingdom of God. Pastor Robertson reveals what uncommon leadership is and clearly defines a method that these agents of change use to facilitate change for the good within any organization. This book will help us to understand that God prepares a leader and thus defines what a leader in the church should be, not the Elders, the Deacons, the Trustees, or any other organizational leaders within the church. To truly embrace the concepts of uncommon leader, we must accept the reality of the scriptures that "God alone creates, sanctifies unto him, God alone calls, and God alone appoints leaders after his own heart. Mere men cannot appoint true biblical leadership." Let's open up the pages of this book and explore what the church has been yearning for, and is now experiencing. A paradigm shift has taken place in church leadership and uncommon leaders have taken their rightful place leading the church into the next span of time.

Chapter 1
I Didn't Ask for This

A leader, who me? I can recall a time in my life where I often responded with a laugh every time that I would hear the word leader, but why was everyone seeing the same thing? Was there something about me that even I did not realize or know? Was I different? Why did I always stand out in a crowd? Could it be that there was something about my personality that causes people to single me out? Well, I wasn't sure, but what I was sure of is that I didn't ask for this!

Over the years I have filled many roles as the person in charge of an organization. It all started at Sumter High School when one of my AFJROTC instructors by the name of MSgt. Jolly spotted something in me that I

Chapter 1

never knew existed. He was one of the first people to recognize my ability to always be out front, taking charge of every situation that I found myself in whether good or bad. What was it that he saw in me? I didn't really know at the time, but MSgt, Jolly called me a "leader." My first thought was, who me? The second was, what does that mean? He explained that I had a natural ability to take charge, and I laughed because my siblings always called me bossy. Is this why I often stood out amongst my peers? Is this the thing that people kept seeing in me that always led me to the front? I guess so, let's look a little further back.

Even though I was the tenth child born to Walter and Janie Robertson, I seemed to always find myself either hanging with my older sister Gloria or hanging out in Rev. Watkins barbershop talking to him and sweeping the floor. For some reason, I always wanted to hang around older people, which was unheard of in the 70' and 80's because a child's place was not in the presence of adults. For some reason, I was permitted to hang around. Unknowingly to my elders I was observing their actions, listening to their advice, and allowing my malleable mind and personality to be molded and prepared for greatness. As a result of the early years of hanging out with either my older siblings or around my friend's grandparents, my friends begin to call me "the old man." Their attempt to mock me was merely revealing my ability to talk sense into them when they were about to do something wrong. I knew then that there was something, uncommon about me because I didn't act or think like the average little boy. Now standing in front of MSgt. Jolly and being called a leader ignited something inside of me that transformed my life.

Within a year or two I was named the commander of the drill team, and eventually one of two squadron commanders in charge of the student cadets who made up SC-21, the AFJROTC Wing at Sumter High School. Later on, I would become a team leader over a shift where I worked, the assistant manager, store manager, director of a homeless shelter, and eventually a pastor. The amazing thing about this journey is that on every step of my progression I was always the uncommon candidate because everyone thought the position would be given to someone else. However, every time there was someone present who noticed the natural ability in me to lead that MSgt. Jolly first identified, yes this is what I called uncommon leadership. In other words, I did not ask to be a leader, and I never expected anyone to identify me as such. I actually thought that I was blending in with everyone else.

Let's explore this a little further, uncommon leaders never ask nor seek to become leaders, but God destines them for greatness. Moses never asked to become the leader of the nation Israel, nonetheless God chose him. Another person who never asked to be a leader was Joseph, yet in every place Joseph found himself, he found favor with God to lead.

In both cases it was uncommon for anyone who was not Egyptian born to lead, but both of these men were placed in position to lead by God. God spared Moses for a greater purpose as he was born during a time where he should have been killed with all of the other Hebrew babies. What was that pur-

Chapter 1

pose? God was raising up uncommon leaders to placed amongst the people. To my amazement God chose me and he is still choosing others to lead his people in an uncommon manner unto this day.

Self-Reflection

What stood out in this chapter?

_____

_____

_____

_____

_____

_____

_____

_____

_____

_____

_____

_____

_____

_____

_____

_____

_____

_____

_____

What personal connection did you make or what behaviors did you find similar to yours?

_____

_____

_____

_____

_____

_____

_____

_____

_____

_____

_____

_____

_____

_____

_____

_____

_____

_____

What will you apply on your leadership journey?

_____

_____

_____

_____

_____

_____

_____

_____

_____

_____

_____

_____

_____

_____

_____

_____

_____

_____

How will you challenge yourself to become
a better leader?

_____

_____

_____

_____

_____

_____

_____

_____

_____

_____

_____

_____

_____

_____

_____

_____

Chapter 2

What is Uncommon Leadership?

Let's start with my personal definition of leadership; leadership is having the ability to yield the power of influence to leverage the knowledge, skills, and abilities of others to maximize the productivity of the organization in order to achieve the goal. Whew, I know that's a rather comprehensive definition, but it is one that I came up with after serving years in various leadership roles. Notice that nowhere in that definition did you find the words "carbon copy." Why? Because you are not meant to copy anyone else's style no matter how many seminars, conferences, or leadership workshops that you attend. You were meant to be an original. It's ok to model some of your methods after the best, but you have to make the behaviors that you chose to model fit your personality and style of leadership. To find out what I mean let's take a look at another uncommon leader in comparison to Moses. The people were used to Moses, it was Moses who led them out of Egypt, It was Moses who led them across the sea, and it was Moses who led them through the wilderness so naturally they were looking for another Moses. Here's the problem that the people created by looking for another Moses, God selected Joshua. Joshua could never be Moses even if he tried, and the truth is God created him to be Joshua. Moses is dead, you can only be who God created you to be.

As a Pastor I would often hear in the church, "our old Pastor never did it that way, etc..." Have you ever heard one of those many excuses? Yes, I said excuses because in the church we make excuses when we are reluctant to embrace new leadership. So why is it that in the church we want our new pastor to be just like our old pastor, can it be that we are under the influence of a spirit of familiarity? Familiarity will cause you to become comfortable in a thing regardless of whether it's being done the right or the wrong way. One thing that I discovered while in leadership is that the church is the only organization that I've been a part of that expects different results without changing a thing. That comes from an antiquated train of thought that has a lot of churches stuck in the glory of yesteryear while yearning to be a part of the now.

The truth of the matter is a lot churches are stuck because they are guilty of forcing Joshua to become Moses. What does that mean? It means that they force to a new leader to operate just like the old one and as a result change and growth are often stifled. Here's what I mean, because of her inability to move away from the past, churches will often complete the pastoral search process, select a young person with a Joshua spirit, and then force them to be just like Moses. Remember, Joshua will never be Moses! Joshua is an uncommon leader, that person who some say is radical and who is not afraid to try new things. Yet once the one with the Joshua/uncommon spirit is installed as the pastor, someone of influence quickly gives them the rundown on what they better not change, what they better not do, what they better not say, and whose position they better not mess with. Have you ever seen this happen or even experienced it yourself?

If you don't remember anything else from this book please remember that, "Joshua can never be Moses!" No matter how hard they try to turn you into Moses or the previous pastor, you have to remain the one whom God placed that uncommon spirit within that spirit like Joshua's. Joshua stuck his foot in the sand so to speak, and refused to conform to the people's desire for more of Moses when he made this statement in Joshua 25:14, *"And if it is evil in your eyes to serve the Lord, choose this day whom you will serve, whether it be the gods your fathers served in the region beyond the river, or the gods of the Amorites in whose land you dwell. But as for me and my house, we will serve the Lord."* This was Joshua's declaration that I will NOT be like everyone else. He made his choice as a leader and challenged the people to rise up to his level. This is a very important characteristic that uncommon leaders possess; they have the ability to challenge those around them to rise to

Chapter 2

their standards and expectations. So, your assignment is to refuse to conform to what everybody else is doing because what works for them may not necessarily work for you. You are uncommon! So let's take a look at what it means to be an uncommon leader.

An uncommon leader is a person who doesn't fit the normal mold of what everyone else thinks a leader should be. This person will often become a leader in a non-traditional manner; their gifts will push them to the front rather than their last name or to whom they owe favors. An uncommon leader is not swayed by the status quo or the traditional way of doing things. An uncommon leader does not march to the rhythm of their own drum; on the contrary, they march to the rhythm of God. They realize that above all things they have to stay in step with God and not in step with mere men. An uncommon leader has attained a certain level of spiritual maturity and is no longer easily swayed by emotions or the emotional response of others. An uncommon leader in the church is more concerned with pleasing God than with pleasing the people. This is what drives him/her to seem fearless in regards to change. This was that spark, that character trait that was hidden to me; I was uncommon and yearning to live up to my true potential. What about you? Are you yearning for something more? Are you yearning to lead your church or organization to a new place in God? Do you have ideas of change that others may see as radical? If so, then you too are an uncommon leader.

Self-Reflection

What stood out in this chapter?

_____

_____

_____

_____

_____

_____

_____

_____

_____

_____

_____

_____

_____

_____

_____

_____

_____

_____

What personal connection did you make or
behaviors did you find similar to yours?

_____

_____

_____

_____

_____

_____

_____

_____

_____

_____

_____

_____

_____

_____

_____

_____

_____

What will you apply on your leadership journey?

_____

_____

_____

_____

_____

_____

_____

_____

_____

_____

_____

_____

_____

_____

_____

_____

_____

_____

How will you challenge yourself to become a better leader?

_____

_____

_____

_____

_____

_____

_____

_____

_____

_____

_____

_____

_____

_____

_____

_____

_____

_____

Chapter 3

The Process of Change

In my years of leadership, I learned that the biggest mistake any new leader can make is to walk into the office and immediately start making changes. This could result in disaster by leading to chaos and confusion as well as making some feel as though they have been betrayed. Remember you are new to the organization, and they chose you because they really want change. However, how you institute change will determine the level of its success.

Over the years of trial and error I developed a five-step approach to change that you may find familiar. This method of change has been very successful within the church as well as other leadership roles that I have previously filled. The five steps of the "Uncommon Leader," approach to change are 1) Observation, 2) Evaluation, 3) Recommendation, 4) Delegation, and 5) Facilitation.

Observation

Stop, whatever you do, don't make that change now you just got here. Upon arrival in an organization as the leader step back and observe the operations of the organization. Don't offer any comments to those who will either inquire about changes or suggest changes for you to make. Remember this observation is solely for you to take notes because you are still viewed as an outsider at this time; therefore, your opinions will be honest and unbiased. It is very important that you take detailed notes to include names as well as actions taken, etc. During this phase is where you will identify the influencers. These are the people to which everyone listens or follows and it is very important to win over the influencers. Use extreme caution when searching out the influencers because every organization has a gossiper who may appear to be an influencer, but you will quickly discover that they stir up conflict more than anything.

Evaluation

Remember you were not placed there to make friends, you are there to lead. During this time, you are reviewing notes and observing visually to determine the effectiveness of a process and in some cases a person's ability to achieve the organization's goal. Be careful, they are watching you too and it's during this phase where the office politicians will attempt to befriend you. They do this to get close enough to you so that you will reveal your plans, don't fall for it. Take note of their actions because you are still in the observation mode.

Recommendation (The Great Giveaway)

This is the most important of all of the steps because this is when you will put the influencers to work. After you have identified an issue or something that you would like to change, this phrase is where you tie a nice bow around it and give it to an influencer. How do I do that? Well, first you present the idea to them (I call this step baiting the hook) express your sincere concern and why you think the change needs to happen. Next, solicit their opinion (setting the hook), everybody wants to feel valued and involved in the process of change and this is where you let the influencer know how much their opinions mean to you as a leader. Be upfront and tell them that you noticed that it seems as if everyone listens to them (value) and that you would really like their help. Once the hook is set the influencer has now become the bait that you will cast out in order to catch everyone else. A good influencer will win over the other key players who will think that the change is the idea of the influencer and before you know it you will have buy-in.

Delegation

You have to use sound judgment in this phase because this is where you will select the person who will spearhead the change. It may or may not be the influencer, but ask if he/she desire to lead it or even who they think would be best to lead it. Again, you are expressing to the influencer that you place value in his/her opinions. This will result in building a relationship of trust and mutual ownership.

Facilitation

Contrary to what some believe, you do not have to implement change all by yourself. You have already identified the various roles that members of the organization play and know it's time to lead. Remember your assignment is to leverage the Knowledge, Skills, and Abilities of others to maximize the productivity of the organization in order to complete the organization's goal. Your main role now is to follow-up with the person whom you have empowered to lead the charge of completing the assignment.

What's amazing about this model of leadership and why I call it uncommon is most churches aren't used to this approach. In the southeastern part of the country where I reside most churches have a pastor who has his hands in/on everything, this is a man-

Chapter 3

agement skill and is NOT a trait of a leader. An uncommon leader gives away more responsibility than they retain because they understand that it's about the mission of the organization and not about them.

Self-Reflection

What stood out in this chapter?

_____

_____

_____

_____

_____

_____

_____

_____

_____

_____

_____

_____

_____

_____

_____

_____

_____

_____

What personal connection did you make or behaviors that you find similar to yours?

_____

_____

_____

_____

_____

_____

_____

_____

_____

_____

_____

_____

_____

_____

_____

_____

_____

_____

_____

What will you apply on your leadership journey?

_____

_____

_____

_____

_____

_____

_____

_____

_____

_____

_____

_____

_____

_____

_____

_____

_____

_____

How will you challenge yourself to become a better leader?

_____

_____

_____

_____

_____

_____

_____

_____

_____

_____

_____

_____

_____

_____

_____

_____

_____

_____

_____

Chapter 4

Uncommon Places

Look out! There is a journey you will have to take as an uncommon leader and a mind-set that will have to overcome. I call it "Egypt Syndrome." What is that, I am sure you are asking? The Egypt Syndrome is the mental condition of resistance to change you will have to deal with as a leader. This resistance shows up in the form of 1. we have never done this before, 2. we are unsure if this is the right thing to do, and 3. it is the fear of the unknown that causes the people to want to return to the old ways.

God sent an uncommon leader named Moses to lead his people out of Egypt, and you know the story after the onset of the plagues Pharaoh finally agreed to set the Hebrew

Chapter 4

people free. However, God hardens the heart of Pharaoh and he decided that he would pursue the Hebrew people in order to bring them back into captivity. What that meant was that the people had a problem, they found themselves up against the Red Sea, and then the problem got even bigger.

Now the Egypt Syndrome was the response of the people. Let's look at it from the book of Exodus chapter 14:10-12 of the English Standard Version of the bible,

"[10]When Pharaoh drew near, the people of Israel lifted up their eyes, and behold, the Egyptians were marching after them, and they feared greatly. And the people of Israel cried out to the Lord. [11] They said to Moses, "Is it because there are no graves in Egypt that you have taken us away to die in the wilderness? What have you done to us in bringing us out of Egypt? [12] Is not this what

we said to you in Egypt: 'Leave us alone that we may serve the Egyptians'? For it would have been better to serve the Egyptians than to die in the wilderness."

The people prayed for change and after their change began upon encountering the first major problem their instinct was to revert back to the old way of doing things. Be careful, because this mindset will cripple you as a leader if you give in.

Moses responded in an uncommon manner, first quieted the people, then dealt with the fear and uncertainty of change, and he acknowledges the existence of the problems. He then reassured the people that if we stay the course, we will reach our goal. Look at his approach, he didn't panic nor did he rebuke the people. He led them calmly in the face of a challenge. Why? He knew that this was the first of many challenges they would face. An uncommon leader understands that challenges will arise. It is in the face of the challenge that the uncommon leader refuse to give up, but will choose to face the challenge head-on.

The point is that you will find yourself in uncommon places from time to time as a leader of an organization, but what matters most is how you respond when in an unfamiliar place. Don't run back to the old methodology or way of doing things. Think outside the box and challenge yourself and the people whom you lead to view the situation through a new lens. As a leader you must understand that effective change may sometimes be painful. However, effective change is necessary for growth. So, embrace the uncommon places and view them as new horizons that the organization must conquer.

If God brought you to the uncommon place, surely, He will lead you through it.

Another good example of finding yourself in an uncommon place is when the Hebrew people arrived at the city of Jericho while on their journey to the promised land. Here in the midst of their journey was their first encounter with a mighty enemy in a fortified city. Joshua could have panicked and fled in an alternate direction with the people, but in leadership, the best approach to dealing with a large problem is head-on. Joshua, the leader, gave the people specific instructions. Joshua instructed them to march around the wall once a day for six-day, and then on the seventh days, they were instructed to march around the city seven times then raise up a great shout. I can imagine the emotions that the people dealt with, first, they were in a strange place, and second, they were used to

Chapter 4

taking up weapons and fighting when necessary. However, this time something was different, the instructions were uncommon or
not the usual way of dealing with a problem.
Once the people executed the uncommon
plan the plan was successful in the end.

As a leader, you have to be willing to respond to uncommon problems in uncommon
places in an uncommon manner. That's it,
be adventurous and lead without fear and
there will be no limits to what you and the
people can accomplish together. Being an
uncommon leader doesn't necessarily mean
that you are a risk-taker, it simply means
that you are willing to go against the grain
and try something different.

Even Uncommon Leaders Need a Mentor

What gave Joshua this drive as a leader? I
can imagine it was a direct result of studying

under the teachings of an even greater leader. You see, every uncommon leader has proven themself to be a greater follower. Joshua spent time learning from Moses' experiences before he was ever allowed to lead. The relationships you form over the years will mold your leadership style by teaching you what to do as well as what not to do. What I mean is learn what works and also what doesn't work from your mentor as you develop into a leader, and then make sure that you maintain a strong network of mentors who will pour into you.

Dr. Shirrie B. Miller who is one of my personal mentors in leadership said, "**You have to be around people who will support and push you to lead.**" She has proven this by pushing me to continue to develop my leadership abilities once I became an educator. She identified my skill set and provided me with many opportunities to develop and practice those skills under her watchful eye. She embraced my uncommon ideas and implemented many of them as we both strived to improve the quality of instruction as well as the experiences of the students at the school.

What is amazing about this mentor/mentee relationship is that she unselfishly pours knowledge of both her failures and her success in leadership into me in order to facilitate my growth. You see, a good mentor is not afraid of failures and understands that failures are mere building blocks in the life of a mentee. I am sure that Joshua heard of the mistakes that Moses made as he was being groomed to be his replacement. Every great mentor will open their lives to be read and studied like an instruction manual in order to assist the one following them on the path of growth in leadership and personal development. Please take note that a good mentor will not attempt to turn you into a carbon copy. Instead a great mentor will allow you to become an original masterpiece under their tutelage.

Self-Reflection

What stood out in this chapter?

_____

_____

_____

_____

_____

_____

_____

_____

_____

_____

_____

_____

_____

_____

_____

_____

_____

_____

_____

_____

What personal connection did you make or behaviors that you find similar to yours?

_____

_____

_____

_____

_____

_____

_____

_____

_____

_____

_____

_____

_____

_____

_____

_____

_____

_____

_____

_____

What will you apply on your leadership journey?

_____

_____

_____

_____

_____

_____

_____

_____

_____

_____

_____

_____

_____

_____

_____

_____

_____

_____

How will you challenge yourself to become
a better leader?

_____

_____

_____

_____

_____

_____

_____

_____

_____

_____

_____

_____

_____

_____

_____

_____

_____

_____

Chapter 5

The Plight of the Uncommon Leader

When your leadership style lands outside of what everyone else around you view as the norm, you will often find yourself in awkward situations. What I mean is while everyone is looking at you thinking "What's wrong with you," you are looking back and thinking, "What's wrong with them?" You will be called different, strange, and my favorite one, radical by other leaders. Why? Is it because I know that I wasn't created to be like everyone else and I embrace the uniqueness of my personality, ability, skills, and knowledge?

Here's a nugget of thought that you need to hold onto, "It's okay to be different and to stand out." Imagine how Jesus must have felt after he stood up in the temple and read from the Book of Isaiah. The Gospel according to Luke 4:20-21tells the story of what Jesus read on that day like this, *"The Spirit of the Lord is upon me, because he has anointed me to preach the gospel to the poor; he has sent me to heal the broken-hearted, to proclaim liberty to the captives and recovery of sight to the blind, to set at liberty those who are oppressed. To preach the acceptable year of the Lord. Then he closed the book, and gave it back to the attendant and sat down. And the eyes of all who were in the synagogue were fixed on him. And he began to say to them, Today this scripture is fulfilled in your hearing."*

The problem was not the particular passages of scripture that Jesus had read because there were many before him who had read the exact same scriptures before. Look

Chapter 5

closely, the people who were present sat pa-
tiently and waited for him to expound on the
meaning of the text, but he shocked them to
their cores by saying, "Today this scripture
is fulfilled in your hearing." On that day the
synagogue was filled with many Scribes and
Pharisees, who were the religious leaders of
that time, and Jesus announced that he was
not like any of them; he made a public con-
fession that he was an Uncommon Leader.
What made him uncommon was that he refused to be assimilated and because of this
he was despised and rejected by other leaders who referred to him as a radical. You
will not be invited into every circle because
some won't be in agreement with how you
are leading the people, but that's okay don't
despise rejection. Jesus was both despised
and rejected. Therefore, when they call you
radical for being uncommon, get excited be-

cause you've just been counted in the same category as Jesus!

I said all of that to say don't be ashamed of who you are as a leader who doesn't fit everyone else's mold. The world, especially the church, is looking for new ideas, new methodology, and a fresh vision. They are looking for uncommon leaders to lead them to uncommon places in an uncommon manner, and you are that leader who dares to stand out in a crowd. You can no longer hide, your gift has brought you into the presence of greatness and their assignment is to help you become even greater than they are. Are you up to the task? Will you answer God's call to lead his people in a new and refreshing way? If your answer is yes, then today is the first day of your uncommon journey. May you walk this journey with boldness,

Chapter 5

strength, and a consistent yearning for more of God's presence.

Self-Reflection

What stood out in this chapter?

_____

_____

_____

_____

_____

_____

_____

_____

_____

_____

_____

_____

_____

_____

_____

_____

_____

_____

What personal connection did you make or
behaviors that you find similar to yours?

_____

_____

_____

_____

_____

_____

_____

_____

_____

_____

_____

_____

_____

_____

_____

_____

_____

What will you apply on your leadership journey?

_____

_____

_____

_____

_____

_____

_____

_____

_____

_____

_____

_____

_____

_____

_____

_____

_____

_____

_____

How will you challenge yourself to become
a better leader?

_____

_____

_____

_____

_____

_____

_____

_____

_____

_____

_____

_____

_____

_____

_____

_____

_____

_____

_____

Chapter 6

Uncommon Discovery

One of the most crippling things when leading people is the struggle with identity crisis, or dealing with the persona of the "average Joe." This means helping people figure out who they are and of what they are capable. During my period of observation, I noticed an individual. In the church she naturally took charge. I evaluated her and noticed that she consistently pursued excellence and completed assignments while inspiring others so effortlessly. I knew immediately that I discovered my first uncommon leader, but when I approached her and told her what I observed and that I wanted her to work alongside me in a leadership role the response was, "not me I'm just an average Joe. I'm nobody, pick somebody else." My response to her was, well that's good to know. The Lord didn't reveal to me what he placed in Joe, but he did reveal to me what he placed into you and he gifted you to lead. From this brief exchange I realized that old average Joe was keeping her from embracing who God said.

Who told Joe that he was average? The word average was first used in the late 15th century to describe goods that were lost at sea. It wasn't until the late 18th century until the word average began to be associated with a degree of measure and ultimately it began to be used as a measurement or gauge of the abilities of people; thus, the rise of the "Average Joe." When the word average precedes a person's name, it becomes descriptive or an adjective. As an adjective, the word average means having the qualities that are seen as typical of a particular person or

thing; mediocre, not very good. This definition is completely contrary to the character
traits that we discovered in Psalms 139.
What does all of that mean to me? If you are
reading this book, then you have already
proven that you are exceptional and not like
the typical person because you are making
an investment in yourself to grow your
knowledge or you are becoming self-aware.
Now your assignment is to help others become self-aware or accept the fact that they
too are uncommon.

So, can Joe and other uncommon people in
the church or any organization overcome the
mindset of being average? Yes, by accepting
their uniqueness and exceptionality. What
do I mean by uniqueness and exceptionality?
Let's look at how the Psalmist speaks of
these two traits of uncommon people, in
Psalms 139:14 (English Standard Version),

"I praise you, for I am fearfully and wonder-fully made. Wonderful are your works; my soul knows it very well." We were not meant to be just like everybody else! Our creator did not use a copy machine to make our physical appearance the same as everyone else. Just in case you're asking yourself, what about identical twins. That description in itself is oxymoronic or it contradicts itself. Although they share a high degree of similarities including birth date and physical appearance, each one still maintains a certain degree of uniqueness that enables everyone else to be able to tell them apart. Therefore, every one of us is a unique individual and no one is average at all. You are fearfully and wonderfully made and God has crowned you with righteousness. You are one of a kind and should never allow yourself to be compared to another person. Why? Jonathan McReynolds said it best, "compar-

ison kills." Kills what, creativity, ingenuity, and dreams.

As a leader you do the organization that you lead a disservice by striving to make them become like someone else. You can admire what other organizations have achieved or have become, but strive to duplicate their success and not duplicate them as an organization. Your organization is unique, dare to be different and uncommon. Do as Robert Frost alludes to in his poem "*Road Not Taken*," when you reach the point where two roads diverge, take the one less traveled. You were not called to leadership in order to become a cookie-cutter leader who does the exact thing that everyone else is doing, dare to be different.

The goal of an uncommon leader and thus my goal as a leader was to help this young

Chapter 6

lady, as well as others, embrace the fact that we each have unique and exceptional knowledge, skills, and abilities that when used properly will make the individual as well as the organization uncommon, unique and exceptional. How did I accomplish this? You just read it in the previous paragraphs. You and I can only share with others who and what God says they are and then help them to embrace their new reality. "I am Uncommon, different and proud to be," so please don't compare me to anyone else.

I am unique! I am exceptional! I am UN-COMMON!

Self-Reflection

What stood out in this chapter?

_____

_____

_____

_____

_____

_____

_____

_____

_____

_____

_____

_____

_____

_____

_____

_____

_____

_____

_____

_____

What personal connection did you make or
behaviors did you find similar to yours?

_____

_____

_____

_____

_____

_____

_____

_____

_____

_____

_____

_____

_____

_____

_____

_____

_____

_____

What will you apply on your leadership journey?

_____

_____

_____

_____

_____

_____

_____

_____

_____

_____

_____

_____

_____

_____

_____

_____

_____

_____

_____

_____

How will you challenge yourself to become
a better leader?

_____

_____

_____

_____

_____

_____

_____

_____

_____

_____

_____

_____

_____

_____

_____

_____

_____

_____

Chapter 7

It's OK To Be Uncommon

After reflecting upon all of this the one thing that I had to accept is that it is OK to be uncommon. God did not create a world of carbon copies. That means we were not designed nor created to be just alike, and if we were all created to look different, then surely, we were created to lead differently.

As a leader, your path to success is predicated upon your ability to embrace who God has created you to be while refusing to allow others to force you to be someone or something else. Accept the fact that not everyone will accept you or your leadership style; therefore, connect with those who will follow you while praying for and working with others who are a part of the organization who are struggling with change. Remember, it is God's desire that not a single one be left behind according to 2 Peter 3:9 English Standard Version, so teach one to reach one. If you build the key people and empower

Chapter 7

them to build up others, then the transition to your leadership style will be embraced by the people.

So, I challenge you once again:

- to lead without limits

- to dare to be unique

- to never be afraid to try new things

- to always be willing to give away credit for an idea

- to see the greatness in all whom you lead (even the ones who frustrate you)

- to never quit!

Always remember that you are an UN-COMMON LEADER who was created to lead on this uncommon way.

Self-Reflection

What stood out in this chapter?

_____

_____

_____

_____

_____

_____

_____

_____

_____

_____

_____

_____

_____

_____

_____

_____

_____

_____

_____

_____

What personal connection did you make or behaviors did you find similar to yours?

_____

_____

_____

_____

_____

_____

_____

_____

_____

_____

_____

_____

_____

_____

_____

_____

_____

_____

_____

What will you apply on your leadership journey?

_____

_____

_____

_____

_____

_____

_____

_____

_____

_____

_____

_____

_____

_____

_____

_____

_____

_____

How will you challenge yourself to become
a better leader?

_____

_____

_____

_____

_____

_____

_____

_____

_____

_____

_____

_____

_____

_____

_____

_____

_____

_____

_____

_____

About the Author

Walter Robertson, III, a School Counselor and Pastor, has a passion for and a genuine love for all children of God. He believes that we all need to be encouraged and lifted up from time to time, especially during the tough times in our lives. He has dedicated his life and ministry to uplifting people as his mission is "to call people's lives back to order." He pastors the Union Baptist Church of Rembert, SC Inc. which is fast growing and thriving spiritually under his leadership.

About the Author

Pastor Robertson hopes that the words of

UNCOMMON Leadership: What the Church Needs Most will challenge others to take a unique and refreshing approach to ministry as they strive to do it God's way and NOT the way that it's always been done.

Other works by Pastor Robertson include "A Product of Grace: Devotions from the Heart of a Pastor," and other books are yet to come.